THIS HOUSE HUNTING JOURNAL BELONGS TO

CONTACT DETAILS

DEDICATION

This House Hunting Journal Log book is dedicated to all the people out there who are in search of a new home and want to document their findings in the process.

You are my inspiration for producing books and I'm honored to be a part of keeping all of your House Hunting notes and records organized.

This journal notebook will help you record your details about finding a new home.

Thoughtfully put together with these sections to record:

Location, Agent Contact Info, Date For Viewing, Prices, Square Foot, Rooms, Floors, Year Built, Does It Have (checklist), Renovation Needed, and much more!

HOW TO USE THIS BOOK

The purpose of this book is to keep all of your House Hunting notes all in one place. It will help keep you organized.

This House Hunting Checklist Journal will allow you to accurately document every detail about finding a new home. It's a great way to chart your course through your purchase of a new home.

Here are examples of the prompts for you to fill in and write about your experience in this book:

1. **Location** - Addresses of the property.

2. **Agent & Contact Info** - Write address & phone number.

3. **Date For Viewing** - When you inspected the property.

4. **Prices** - Final asking price of the seller.

5. **Square Foot** - How many square feet.

6. **Rooms** - How many rooms there are.

7. **Floors** - What style of house, how many floors.

8. **Year Built** - When it was built.

9. **Does It Have** - (Check list boxes to check if it has Balcony, Garden, Parking, Garage, Swimming Pool, Built In Closet, Appliances, Etc)

10. **Renovations Needed**

11. **Overall Condition** - Room for writing your rating of the property.

12. **What I Liked** - Lots of space for notes on what you liked about the property.

13. **What I Didn't Like** - Lots of space for notes on what you didn't like about the property.

LOCATION _____

AGENT _____ **CONTACT NO.** _____

DATE FOR VIEWING _____

PRICE _____ **SQM** _____

ROOMS _____ **FLOORS** _____

YEAR BUILT _____

☐ BALCONY   **RENOVATIONS NEEDED**

☐ GARDEN   ☐

☐ PARKING   ☐

☐ GARAGE   ☐

☐ SWIMMING POOL   ☐

☐ BUILT IN CLOSET ☐

☐ APPLIANCES   ☐

☐ PORCH   ☐

OVERALL CONDITION
_____

WHAT I LIKED   **WHAT I DIDN'T LIKE**
_____
_____
_____
_____
_____
_____

LOCATION

AGENT   CONTACT NO.

DATE FOR VIEWING

PRICE   SQM

ROOMS   FLOORS

YEAR BUILT

- ☐ BALCONY   RENOVATIONS NEEDED
- ☐ GARDEN   ☐
- ☐ PARKING   ☐
- ☐ GARAGE   ☐
- ☐ SWIMMING POOL   ☐
- ☐ BUILT IN CLOSET   ☐
- ☐ APPLIANCES   ☐
- ☐ PORCH   ☐

OVERALL CONDITION

WHAT I LIKED   WHAT I DIDN'T LIKE

LOCATION

AGENT   **CONTACT NO.**

DATE FOR VIEWING

PRICE   **SQM**

ROOMS   **FLOORS**

YEAR BUILT

- [ ] BALCONY   **RENOVATIONS NEEDED**
- [ ] GARDEN   [ ]
- [ ] PARKING   [ ]
- [ ] GARAGE   [ ]
- [ ] SWIMMING POOL   [ ]
- [ ] BUILT IN CLOSET   [ ]
- [ ] APPLIANCES   [ ]
- [ ] PORCH   [ ]

OVERALL CONDITION

WHAT I LIKED	WHAT I DIDN'T LIKE

LOCATION

AGENT   CONTACT NO.

DATE FOR VIEWING

PRICE   SQM

ROOMS   FLOORS

YEAR BUILT

☐ BALCONY   RENOVATIONS NEEDED

☐ GARDEN   ☐

☐ PARKING   ☐

☐ GARAGE   ☐

☐ SWIMMING POOL   ☐

☐ BUILT IN CLOSET   ☐

☐ APPLIANCES   ☐

☐ PORCH   ☐

OVERALL CONDITION

WHAT I LIKED   WHAT I DIDN'T LIKE

LOCATION

AGENT   CONTACT NO.

DATE FOR VIEWING

PRICE   SQM

ROOMS   FLOORS

YEAR BUILT

☐ BALCONY   RENOVATIONS NEEDED
☐ GARDEN   ☐
☐ PARKING   ☐
☐ GARAGE   ☐
☐ SWIMMING POOL   ☐
☐ BUILT IN CLOSET ☐
☐ APPLIANCES   ☐
☐ PORCH   ☐

OVERALL CONDITION

WHAT I LIKED   WHAT I DIDN'T LIKE

LOCATION

AGENT   CONTACT NO.

DATE FOR VIEWING

PRICE   SQM

ROOMS   FLOORS

YEAR BUILT

☐ BALCONY   RENOVATIONS NEEDED

☐ GARDEN   ☐

☐ PARKING   ☐

☐ GARAGE   ☐

☐ SWIMMING POOL   ☐

☐ BUILT IN CLOSET ☐

☐ APPLIANCES   ☐

☐ PORCH   ☐

OVERALL CONDITION

WHAT I LIKED   WHAT I DIDN'T LIKE

LOCATION

AGENT   **CONTACT NO.**

DATE FOR VIEWING

PRICE   **SQM**

ROOMS   **FLOORS**

YEAR BUILT

☐ **BALCONY**   **RENOVATIONS NEEDED**

☐ **GARDEN**   ☐

☐ **PARKING**   ☐

☐ **GARAGE**   ☐

☐ **SWIMMING POOL**   ☐

☐ **BUILT IN CLOSET**   ☐

☐ **APPLIANCES**   ☐

☐ **PORCH**   ☐

OVERALL CONDITION

WHAT I LIKED   **WHAT I DIDN'T LIKE**

LOCATION

AGENT   **CONTACT NO.**

DATE FOR VIEWING

PRICE   **SQM**

ROOMS   **FLOORS**

YEAR BUILT

☐ BALCONY   **RENOVATIONS NEEDED**

☐ GARDEN   ☐

☐ PARKING   ☐

☐ GARAGE   ☐

☐ SWIMMING POOL   ☐

☐ BUILT IN CLOSET ☐

☐ APPLIANCES   ☐

☐ PORCH   ☐

OVERALL CONDITION

WHAT I LIKED   **WHAT I DIDN'T LIKE**

LOCATION

AGENT   CONTACT NO.

DATE FOR VIEWING

PRICE   SQM

ROOMS   FLOORS

YEAR BUILT

☐ BALCONY   RENOVATIONS NEEDED
☐ GARDEN   ☐
☐ PARKING   ☐
☐ GARAGE   ☐
☐ SWIMMING POOL   ☐
☐ BUILT IN CLOSET   ☐
☐ APPLIANCES   ☐
☐ PORCH   ☐

OVERALL CONDITION

WHAT I LIKED   WHAT I DIDN'T LIKE

LOCATION

AGENT   CONTACT NO.

DATE FOR VIEWING

PRICE   SQM

ROOMS   FLOORS

YEAR BUILT

☐ BALCONY   RENOVATIONS NEEDED

☐ GARDEN   ☐

☐ PARKING   ☐

☐ GARAGE   ☐

☐ SWIMMING POOL   ☐

☐ BUILT IN CLOSET   ☐

☐ APPLIANCES   ☐

☐ PORCH   ☐

OVERALL CONDITION

WHAT I LIKED   WHAT I DIDN'T LIKE

LOCATION

AGENT   **CONTACT NO.**

DATE FOR VIEWING

PRICE   **SQM**

ROOMS   **FLOORS**

YEAR BUILT

☐ **BALCONY**   **RENOVATIONS NEEDED**

☐ **GARDEN**   ☐

☐ **PARKING**   ☐

☐ **GARAGE**   ☐

☐ **SWIMMING POOL**   ☐

☐ **BUILT IN CLOSET**   ☐

☐ **APPLIANCES**   ☐

☐ **PORCH**   ☐

OVERALL CONDITION

WHAT I LIKED   **WHAT I DIDN'T LIKE**

LOCATION

AGENT   CONTACT NO.

DATE FOR VIEWING

PRICE   SQM

ROOMS   FLOORS

YEAR BUILT

☐ BALCONY   RENOVATIONS NEEDED
☐ GARDEN   ☐
☐ PARKING   ☐
☐ GARAGE   ☐
☐ SWIMMING POOL   ☐
☐ BUILT IN CLOSET   ☐
☐ APPLIANCES   ☐
☐ PORCH   ☐

OVERALL CONDITION

WHAT I LIKED   WHAT I DIDN'T LIKE

LOCATION

AGENT   **CONTACT NO.**

DATE FOR VIEWING

PRICE   **SQM**

ROOMS   **FLOORS**

YEAR BUILT

☐ **BALCONY**   **RENOVATIONS NEEDED**

☐ **GARDEN**   ☐

☐ **PARKING**   ☐

☐ **GARAGE**   ☐

☐ **SWIMMING POOL**   ☐

☐ **BUILT IN CLOSET**   ☐

☐ **APPLIANCES**   ☐

☐ **PORCH**   ☐

OVERALL CONDITION

WHAT I LIKED   **WHAT I DIDN'T LIKE**

LOCATION

AGENT   **CONTACT NO.**

DATE FOR VIEWING

PRICE   **SQM**

ROOMS   **FLOORS**

YEAR BUILT

☐ BALCONY   **RENOVATIONS NEEDED**

☐ GARDEN   ☐

☐ PARKING   ☐

☐ GARAGE   ☐

☐ SWIMMING POOL   ☐

☐ BUILT IN CLOSET   ☐

☐ APPLIANCES   ☐

☐ PORCH   ☐

OVERALL CONDITION

WHAT I LIKED   **WHAT I DIDN'T LIKE**

LOCATION

AGENT   CONTACT NO.

DATE FOR VIEWING

PRICE   SQM

ROOMS   FLOORS

YEAR BUILT

☐ BALCONY   RENOVATIONS NEEDED
☐ GARDEN   ☐
☐ PARKING   ☐
☐ GARAGE   ☐
☐ SWIMMING POOL   ☐
☐ BUILT IN CLOSET   ☐
☐ APPLIANCES   ☐
☐ PORCH   ☐

OVERALL CONDITION

WHAT I LIKED   WHAT I DIDN'T LIKE

LOCATION

AGENT   **CONTACT NO.**

DATE FOR VIEWING

PRICE   **SQM**

ROOMS   **FLOORS**

YEAR BUILT

- ☐ BALCONY   **RENOVATIONS NEEDED**
- ☐ GARDEN   ☐
- ☐ PARKING   ☐
- ☐ GARAGE   ☐
- ☐ SWIMMING POOL   ☐
- ☐ BUILT IN CLOSET   ☐
- ☐ APPLIANCES   ☐
- ☐ PORCH   ☐

OVERALL CONDITION

WHAT I LIKED   **WHAT I DIDN'T LIKE**

LOCATION

AGENT   **CONTACT NO.**

DATE FOR VIEWING

PRICE   **SQM**

ROOMS   **FLOORS**

YEAR BUILT

☐ BALCONY   **RENOVATIONS NEEDED**

☐ GARDEN   ☐

☐ PARKING   ☐

☐ GARAGE   ☐

☐ SWIMMING POOL   ☐

☐ BUILT IN CLOSET   ☐

☐ APPLIANCES   ☐

☐ PORCH   ☐

OVERALL CONDITION

WHAT I LIKED   **WHAT I DIDN'T LIKE**

LOCATION

AGENT   CONTACT NO.

DATE FOR VIEWING

PRICE   SQM

ROOMS   FLOORS

YEAR BUILT

☐ BALCONY   RENOVATIONS NEEDED

☐ GARDEN   ☐

☐ PARKING   ☐

☐ GARAGE   ☐

☐ SWIMMING POOL   ☐

☐ BUILT IN CLOSET   ☐

☐ APPLIANCES   ☐

☐ PORCH   ☐

OVERALL CONDITION

WHAT I LIKED   WHAT I DIDN'T LIKE

LOCATION

AGENT   **CONTACT NO.**

DATE FOR VIEWING

PRICE   **SQM**

ROOMS   **FLOORS**

YEAR BUILT

☐ BALCONY   **RENOVATIONS NEEDED**

☐ GARDEN   ☐

☐ PARKING   ☐

☐ GARAGE   ☐

☐ SWIMMING POOL   ☐

☐ BUILT IN CLOSET   ☐

☐ APPLIANCES   ☐

☐ PORCH   ☐

OVERALL CONDITION

WHAT I LIKED   **WHAT I DIDN'T LIKE**

LOCATION

AGENT   CONTACT NO.

DATE FOR VIEWING

PRICE   SQM

ROOMS   FLOORS

YEAR BUILT

☐ BALCONY   RENOVATIONS NEEDED
☐ GARDEN   ☐
☐ PARKING   ☐
☐ GARAGE   ☐
☐ SWIMMING POOL   ☐
☐ BUILT IN CLOSET   ☐
☐ APPLIANCES   ☐
☐ PORCH   ☐

OVERALL CONDITION

WHAT I LIKED   WHAT I DIDN'T LIKE

LOCATION

AGENT   **CONTACT NO.**

DATE FOR VIEWING

PRICE   **SQM**

ROOMS   **FLOORS**

YEAR BUILT

- [ ] **BALCONY**   **RENOVATIONS NEEDED**
- [ ] **GARDEN**   [ ]
- [ ] **PARKING**   [ ]
- [ ] **GARAGE**   [ ]
- [ ] **SWIMMING POOL**   [ ]
- [ ] **BUILT IN CLOSET**   [ ]
- [ ] **APPLIANCES**   [ ]
- [ ] **PORCH**   [ ]

OVERALL CONDITION

WHAT I LIKED   **WHAT I DIDN'T LIKE**

LOCATION

AGENT   **CONTACT NO.**

DATE FOR VIEWING

PRICE   **SQM**

ROOMS   **FLOORS**

YEAR BUILT

- ☐ **BALCONY**   **RENOVATIONS NEEDED**
- ☐ **GARDEN** ☐
- ☐ **PARKING** ☐
- ☐ **GARAGE** ☐
- ☐ **SWIMMING POOL** ☐
- ☐ **BUILT IN CLOSET** ☐
- ☐ **APPLIANCES** ☐
- ☐ **PORCH** ☐

OVERALL CONDITION

WHAT I LIKED	**WHAT I DIDN'T LIKE**

LOCATION

AGENT   **CONTACT NO.**

DATE FOR VIEWING

PRICE   **SQM**

ROOMS   **FLOORS**

YEAR BUILT

☐ **BALCONY**   **RENOVATIONS NEEDED**

☐ **GARDEN**   ☐

☐ **PARKING**   ☐

☐ **GARAGE**   ☐

☐ **SWIMMING POOL**   ☐

☐ **BUILT IN CLOSET**   ☐

☐ **APPLIANCES**   ☐

☐ **PORCH**   ☐

OVERALL CONDITION

WHAT I LIKED   **WHAT I DIDN'T LIKE**

LOCATION

AGENT   CONTACT NO.

DATE FOR VIEWING

PRICE   SQM

ROOMS   FLOORS

YEAR BUILT

☐ BALCONY   RENOVATIONS NEEDED
☐ GARDEN   ☐
☐ PARKING   ☐
☐ GARAGE   ☐
☐ SWIMMING POOL   ☐
☐ BUILT IN CLOSET   ☐
☐ APPLIANCES   ☐
☐ PORCH   ☐

OVERALL CONDITION

WHAT I LIKED   WHAT I DIDN'T LIKE

LOCATION

AGENT   **CONTACT NO.**

DATE FOR VIEWING

PRICE   **SQM**

ROOMS   **FLOORS**

YEAR BUILT

☐ BALCONY   **RENOVATIONS NEEDED**

☐ GARDEN   ☐

☐ PARKING   ☐

☐ GARAGE   ☐

☐ SWIMMING POOL   ☐

☐ BUILT IN CLOSET   ☐

☐ APPLIANCES   ☐

☐ PORCH   ☐

OVERALL CONDITION

WHAT I LIKED   **WHAT I DIDN'T LIKE**

LOCATION

AGENT   CONTACT NO.

DATE FOR VIEWING

PRICE   SQM

ROOMS   FLOORS

YEAR BUILT

☐ BALCONY   RENOVATIONS NEEDED

☐ GARDEN   ☐

☐ PARKING   ☐

☐ GARAGE   ☐

☐ SWIMMING POOL   ☐

☐ BUILT IN CLOSET   ☐

☐ APPLIANCES   ☐

☐ PORCH   ☐

OVERALL CONDITION

WHAT I LIKED   WHAT I DIDN'T LIKE

LOCATION

AGENT   CONTACT NO.

DATE FOR VIEWING

PRICE   SQM

ROOMS   FLOORS

YEAR BUILT

☐ BALCONY   RENOVATIONS NEEDED
☐ GARDEN   ☐
☐ PARKING   ☐
☐ GARAGE   ☐
☐ SWIMMING POOL   ☐
☐ BUILT IN CLOSET   ☐
☐ APPLIANCES   ☐
☐ PORCH   ☐

OVERALL CONDITION

WHAT I LIKED   WHAT I DIDN'T LIKE

LOCATION

AGENT   CONTACT NO.

DATE FOR VIEWING

PRICE   SQM

ROOMS   FLOORS

YEAR BUILT

☐ BALCONY   RENOVATIONS NEEDED

☐ GARDEN   ☐

☐ PARKING   ☐

☐ GARAGE   ☐

☐ SWIMMING POOL   ☐

☐ BUILT IN CLOSET   ☐

☐ APPLIANCES   ☐

☐ PORCH   ☐

OVERALL CONDITION

WHAT I LIKED   WHAT I DIDN'T LIKE

LOCATION

AGENT   **CONTACT NO.**

DATE FOR VIEWING

PRICE   **SQM**

ROOMS   **FLOORS**

YEAR BUILT

- [ ] **BALCONY**   **RENOVATIONS NEEDED**
- [ ] **GARDEN**   [ ]
- [ ] **PARKING**   [ ]
- [ ] **GARAGE**   [ ]
- [ ] **SWIMMING POOL**   [ ]
- [ ] **BUILT IN CLOSET**   [ ]
- [ ] **APPLIANCES**   [ ]
- [ ] **PORCH**   [ ]

OVERALL CONDITION

WHAT I LIKED	**WHAT I DIDN'T LIKE**

LOCATION

AGENT   CONTACT NO.

DATE FOR VIEWING

PRICE   SQM

ROOMS   FLOORS

YEAR BUILT

☐ BALCONY   RENOVATIONS NEEDED

☐ GARDEN   ☐

☐ PARKING   ☐

☐ GARAGE   ☐

☐ SWIMMING POOL   ☐

☐ BUILT IN CLOSET   ☐

☐ APPLIANCES   ☐

☐ PORCH   ☐

OVERALL CONDITION

WHAT I LIKED   WHAT I DIDN'T LIKE

LOCATION

AGENT   **CONTACT NO.**

DATE FOR VIEWING

PRICE   **SQM**

ROOMS   **FLOORS**

YEAR BUILT

☐ BALCONY   **RENOVATIONS NEEDED**

☐ GARDEN   ☐

☐ PARKING   ☐

☐ GARAGE   ☐

☐ SWIMMING POOL   ☐

☐ BUILT IN CLOSET   ☐

☐ APPLIANCES   ☐

☐ PORCH   ☐

OVERALL CONDITION

WHAT I LIKED   **WHAT I DIDN'T LIKE**

LOCATION

AGENT   CONTACT NO.

DATE FOR VIEWING

PRICE   SQM

ROOMS   FLOORS

YEAR BUILT

☐ BALCONY   RENOVATIONS NEEDED
☐ GARDEN   ☐
☐ PARKING   ☐
☐ GARAGE   ☐
☐ SWIMMING POOL   ☐
☐ BUILT IN CLOSET   ☐
☐ APPLIANCES   ☐
☐ PORCH   ☐

OVERALL CONDITION

WHAT I LIKED   WHAT I DIDN'T LIKE

LOCATION

AGENT   CONTACT NO.

DATE FOR VIEWING

PRICE   SQM

ROOMS   FLOORS

YEAR BUILT

☐ BALCONY   RENOVATIONS NEEDED
☐ GARDEN   ☐
☐ PARKING   ☐
☐ GARAGE   ☐
☐ SWIMMING POOL   ☐
☐ BUILT IN CLOSET ☐
☐ APPLIANCES   ☐
☐ PORCH   ☐

OVERALL CONDITION

WHAT I LIKED   WHAT I DIDN'T LIKE

LOCATION

AGENT   CONTACT NO.

DATE FOR VIEWING

PRICE   SQM

ROOMS   FLOORS

YEAR BUILT

- [ ] BALCONY   RENOVATIONS NEEDED
- [ ] GARDEN   [ ]
- [ ] PARKING   [ ]
- [ ] GARAGE   [ ]
- [ ] SWIMMING POOL   [ ]
- [ ] BUILT IN CLOSET   [ ]
- [ ] APPLIANCES   [ ]
- [ ] PORCH   [ ]

OVERALL CONDITION

WHAT I LIKED   WHAT I DIDN'T LIKE

LOCATION

AGENT **CONTACT NO.**

DATE FOR VIEWING

PRICE **SQM**

ROOMS **FLOORS**

YEAR BUILT

☐ BALCONY **RENOVATIONS NEEDED**

☐ GARDEN ☐

☐ PARKING ☐

☐ GARAGE ☐

☐ SWIMMING POOL ☐

☐ BUILT IN CLOSET ☐

☐ APPLIANCES ☐

☐ PORCH ☐

OVERALL CONDITION

WHAT I LIKED **WHAT I DIDN'T LIKE**

LOCATION
_____

AGENT   CONTACT NO.
_____

DATE FOR VIEWING
_____

PRICE   SQM
_____

ROOMS   FLOORS
_____

YEAR BUILT
_____

☐ BALCONY   RENOVATIONS NEEDED

☐ GARDEN   ☐

☐ PARKING   ☐

☐ GARAGE   ☐

☐ SWIMMING POOL   ☐

☐ BUILT IN CLOSET   ☐

☐ APPLIANCES   ☐

☐ PORCH   ☐

OVERALL CONDITION
_____

WHAT I LIKED   WHAT I DIDN'T LIKE
_____

_____

_____

_____

_____

_____

LOCATION

AGENT   **CONTACT NO.**

DATE FOR VIEWING

PRICE   **SQM**

ROOMS   **FLOORS**

YEAR BUILT

☐ BALCONY   **RENOVATIONS NEEDED**

☐ GARDEN   ☐

☐ PARKING   ☐

☐ GARAGE   ☐

☐ SWIMMING POOL   ☐

☐ BUILT IN CLOSET   ☐

☐ APPLIANCES   ☐

☐ PORCH   ☐

OVERALL CONDITION

WHAT I LIKED   **WHAT I DIDN'T LIKE**

LOCATION

AGENT **CONTACT NO.**

DATE FOR VIEWING

PRICE **SQM**

ROOMS **FLOORS**

YEAR BUILT

- ☐ BALCONY **RENOVATIONS NEEDED**
- ☐ GARDEN ☐
- ☐ PARKING ☐
- ☐ GARAGE ☐
- ☐ SWIMMING POOL ☐
- ☐ BUILT IN CLOSET ☐
- ☐ APPLIANCES ☐
- ☐ PORCH ☐

OVERALL CONDITION

WHAT I LIKED **WHAT I DIDN'T LIKE**

LOCATION

AGENT   **CONTACT NO.**

DATE FOR VIEWING

PRICE   **SQM**

ROOMS   **FLOORS**

YEAR BUILT

- ☐ **BALCONY**   **RENOVATIONS NEEDED**
- ☐ **GARDEN**   ☐
- ☐ **PARKING**   ☐
- ☐ **GARAGE**   ☐
- ☐ **SWIMMING POOL**   ☐
- ☐ **BUILT IN CLOSET**   ☐
- ☐ **APPLIANCES**   ☐
- ☐ **PORCH**   ☐

OVERALL CONDITION

WHAT I LIKED	WHAT I DIDN'T LIKE

LOCATION

AGENT   CONTACT NO.

DATE FOR VIEWING

PRICE   SQM

ROOMS   FLOORS

YEAR BUILT

☐ BALCONY   RENOVATIONS NEEDED

☐ GARDEN   ☐

☐ PARKING   ☐

☐ GARAGE   ☐

☐ SWIMMING POOL   ☐

☐ BUILT IN CLOSET   ☐

☐ APPLIANCES   ☐

☐ PORCH   ☐

OVERALL CONDITION

WHAT I LIKED   WHAT I DIDN'T LIKE

LOCATION

AGENT   **CONTACT NO.**

DATE FOR VIEWING

PRICE   **SQM**

ROOMS   **FLOORS**

YEAR BUILT

☐ **BALCONY**   **RENOVATIONS NEEDED**

☐ **GARDEN**   ☐

☐ **PARKING**   ☐

☐ **GARAGE**   ☐

☐ **SWIMMING POOL**   ☐

☐ **BUILT IN CLOSET**   ☐

☐ **APPLIANCES**   ☐

☐ **PORCH**   ☐

OVERALL CONDITION

WHAT I LIKED   **WHAT I DIDN'T LIKE**

LOCATION

AGENT CONTACT NO.

DATE FOR VIEWING

PRICE SQM

ROOMS FLOORS

YEAR BUILT

- [ ] BALCONY
- [ ] GARDEN
- [ ] PARKING
- [ ] GARAGE
- [ ] SWIMMING POOL
- [ ] BUILT IN CLOSET
- [ ] APPLIANCES
- [ ] PORCH

RENOVATIONS NEEDED

- [ ]
- [ ]
- [ ]
- [ ]
- [ ]
- [ ]
- [ ]

OVERALL CONDITION

WHAT I LIKED WHAT I DIDN'T LIKE

LOCATION

AGENT   CONTACT NO.

DATE FOR VIEWING

PRICE   SQM

ROOMS   FLOORS

YEAR BUILT

☐ BALCONY   RENOVATIONS NEEDED
☐ GARDEN   ☐
☐ PARKING   ☐
☐ GARAGE   ☐
☐ SWIMMING POOL   ☐
☐ BUILT IN CLOSET   ☐
☐ APPLIANCES   ☐
☐ PORCH   ☐

OVERALL CONDITION

WHAT I LIKED   WHAT I DIDN'T LIKE

LOCATION

AGENT   CONTACT NO.

DATE FOR VIEWING

PRICE   SQM

ROOMS   FLOORS

YEAR BUILT

☐ BALCONY   RENOVATIONS NEEDED

☐ GARDEN   ☐

☐ PARKING   ☐

☐ GARAGE   ☐

☐ SWIMMING POOL   ☐

☐ BUILT IN CLOSET   ☐

☐ APPLIANCES   ☐

☐ PORCH   ☐

OVERALL CONDITION

WHAT I LIKED   WHAT I DIDN'T LIKE

LOCATION

AGENT   **CONTACT NO.**

DATE FOR VIEWING

PRICE   **SQM**

ROOMS   **FLOORS**

YEAR BUILT

- ☐ **BALCONY**
- ☐ **GARDEN**
- ☐ **PARKING**
- ☐ **GARAGE**
- ☐ **SWIMMING POOL**
- ☐ **BUILT IN CLOSET**
- ☐ **APPLIANCES**
- ☐ **PORCH**

RENOVATIONS NEEDED

- ☐
- ☐
- ☐
- ☐
- ☐
- ☐
- ☐

OVERALL CONDITION

WHAT I LIKED   **WHAT I DIDN'T LIKE**

LOCATION

AGENT   CONTACT NO.

DATE FOR VIEWING

PRICE   SQM

ROOMS   FLOORS

YEAR BUILT

☐ BALCONY   RENOVATIONS NEEDED

☐ GARDEN   ☐

☐ PARKING   ☐

☐ GARAGE   ☐

☐ SWIMMING POOL ☐

☐ BUILT IN CLOSET ☐

☐ APPLIANCES   ☐

☐ PORCH   ☐

OVERALL CONDITION

WHAT I LIKED   WHAT I DIDN'T LIKE

LOCATION

AGENT   **CONTACT NO.**

DATE FOR VIEWING

PRICE   **SQM**

ROOMS   **FLOORS**

YEAR BUILT

☐ BALCONY   **RENOVATIONS NEEDED**

☐ GARDEN   ☐

☐ PARKING   ☐

☐ GARAGE   ☐

☐ SWIMMING POOL   ☐

☐ BUILT IN CLOSET   ☐

☐ APPLIANCES   ☐

☐ PORCH   ☐

OVERALL CONDITION

WHAT I LIKED   **WHAT I DIDN'T LIKE**

LOCATION

AGENT   **CONTACT NO.**

DATE FOR VIEWING

PRICE   **SQM**

ROOMS   **FLOORS**

YEAR BUILT

☐ **BALCONY**   **RENOVATIONS NEEDED**

☐ **GARDEN**   ☐

☐ **PARKING**   ☐

☐ **GARAGE**   ☐

☐ **SWIMMING POOL**   ☐

☐ **BUILT IN CLOSET**   ☐

☐ **APPLIANCES**   ☐

☐ **PORCH**   ☐

OVERALL CONDITION

WHAT I LIKED   **WHAT I DIDN'T LIKE**

LOCATION

AGENT   CONTACT NO.

DATE FOR VIEWING

PRICE   SQM

ROOMS   FLOORS

YEAR BUILT

☐ BALCONY   RENOVATIONS NEEDED

☐ GARDEN   ☐

☐ PARKING   ☐

☐ GARAGE   ☐

☐ SWIMMING POOL   ☐

☐ BUILT IN CLOSET ☐

☐ APPLIANCES   ☐

☐ PORCH   ☐

OVERALL CONDITION

WHAT I LIKED   WHAT I DIDN'T LIKE

LOCATION

AGENT   CONTACT NO.

DATE FOR VIEWING

PRICE   SQM

ROOMS   FLOORS

YEAR BUILT

☐ BALCONY   RENOVATIONS NEEDED

☐ GARDEN   ☐

☐ PARKING   ☐

☐ GARAGE   ☐

☐ SWIMMING POOL ☐

☐ BUILT IN CLOSET ☐

☐ APPLIANCES   ☐

☐ PORCH   ☐

OVERALL CONDITION

WHAT I LIKED   WHAT I DIDN'T LIKE

LOCATION _____

AGENT _____ CONTACT NO. _____

DATE FOR VIEWING _____

PRICE _____ SQM _____

ROOMS _____ FLOORS _____

YEAR BUILT _____

☐ BALCONY   RENOVATIONS NEEDED
☐ GARDEN   ☐
☐ PARKING   ☐
☐ GARAGE   ☐
☐ SWIMMING POOL   ☐
☐ BUILT IN CLOSET ☐
☐ APPLIANCES   ☐
☐ PORCH   ☐

OVERALL CONDITION
_____

WHAT I LIKED   WHAT I DIDN'T LIKE
_____

_____

_____

_____

_____

_____

LOCATION

AGENT   CONTACT NO.

DATE FOR VIEWING

PRICE   SQM

ROOMS   FLOORS

YEAR BUILT

☐ BALCONY   RENOVATIONS NEEDED

☐ GARDEN   ☐

☐ PARKING   ☐

☐ GARAGE   ☐

☐ SWIMMING POOL   ☐

☐ BUILT IN CLOSET   ☐

☐ APPLIANCES   ☐

☐ PORCH   ☐

OVERALL CONDITION

WHAT I LIKED   WHAT I DIDN'T LIKE

LOCATION

AGENT **CONTACT NO.**

DATE FOR VIEWING

PRICE **SQM**

ROOMS **FLOORS**

YEAR BUILT

- ☐ BALCONY
- ☐ GARDEN
- ☐ PARKING
- ☐ GARAGE
- ☐ SWIMMING POOL
- ☐ BUILT IN CLOSET
- ☐ APPLIANCES
- ☐ PORCH

RENOVATIONS NEEDED

- ☐
- ☐
- ☐
- ☐
- ☐
- ☐
- ☐

OVERALL CONDITION

WHAT I LIKED **WHAT I DIDN'T LIKE**

LOCATION

AGENT   CONTACT NO.

DATE FOR VIEWING

PRICE   SQM

ROOMS   FLOORS

YEAR BUILT

☐ BALCONY   RENOVATIONS NEEDED

☐ GARDEN   ☐

☐ PARKING   ☐

☐ GARAGE   ☐

☐ SWIMMING POOL   ☐

☐ BUILT IN CLOSET   ☐

☐ APPLIANCES   ☐

☐ PORCH   ☐

OVERALL CONDITION

WHAT I LIKED   WHAT I DIDN'T LIKE

LOCATION

AGENT **CONTACT NO.**

DATE FOR VIEWING

PRICE **SQM**

ROOMS **FLOORS**

YEAR BUILT

- ☐ **BALCONY**
- ☐ **GARDEN**
- ☐ **PARKING**
- ☐ **GARAGE**
- ☐ **SWIMMING POOL**
- ☐ **BUILT IN CLOSET**
- ☐ **APPLIANCES**
- ☐ **PORCH**

RENOVATIONS NEEDED

☐
☐
☐
☐
☐
☐
☐

OVERALL CONDITION

WHAT I LIKED **WHAT I DIDN'T LIKE**

LOCATION

AGENT   **CONTACT NO.**

DATE FOR VIEWING

PRICE   **SQM**

ROOMS   **FLOORS**

YEAR BUILT

☐ **BALCONY**   **RENOVATIONS NEEDED**

☐ **GARDEN**   ☐

☐ **PARKING**   ☐

☐ **GARAGE**   ☐

☐ **SWIMMING POOL**   ☐

☐ **BUILT IN CLOSET**   ☐

☐ **APPLIANCES**   ☐

☐ **PORCH**   ☐

OVERALL CONDITION

WHAT I LIKED   **WHAT I DIDN'T LIKE**

LOCATION

AGENT   **CONTACT NO.**

DATE FOR VIEWING

PRICE   **SQM**

ROOMS   **FLOORS**

YEAR BUILT

- ☐ **BALCONY**   **RENOVATIONS NEEDED**
- ☐ **GARDEN**   ☐
- ☐ **PARKING**   ☐
- ☐ **GARAGE**   ☐
- ☐ **SWIMMING POOL**   ☐
- ☐ **BUILT IN CLOSET**   ☐
- ☐ **APPLIANCES**   ☐
- ☐ **PORCH**   ☐

OVERALL CONDITION

WHAT I LIKED	WHAT I DIDN'T LIKE

LOCATION

AGENT   **CONTACT NO.**

DATE FOR VIEWING

PRICE   **SQM**

ROOMS   **FLOORS**

YEAR BUILT

- [ ] BALCONY   **RENOVATIONS NEEDED**
- [ ] GARDEN   [ ]
- [ ] PARKING   [ ]
- [ ] GARAGE   [ ]
- [ ] SWIMMING POOL   [ ]
- [ ] BUILT IN CLOSET   [ ]
- [ ] APPLIANCES   [ ]
- [ ] PORCH   [ ]

OVERALL CONDITION

WHAT I LIKED   **WHAT I DIDN'T LIKE**

LOCATION

AGENT   CONTACT NO.

DATE FOR VIEWING

PRICE   SQM

ROOMS   FLOORS

YEAR BUILT

☐ BALCONY   RENOVATIONS NEEDED
☐ GARDEN   ☐
☐ PARKING   ☐
☐ GARAGE   ☐
☐ SWIMMING POOL   ☐
☐ BUILT IN CLOSET   ☐
☐ APPLIANCES   ☐
☐ PORCH   ☐

OVERALL CONDITION

WHAT I LIKED   WHAT I DIDN'T LIKE

LOCATION

AGENT   CONTACT NO.

DATE FOR VIEWING

PRICE   SQM

ROOMS   FLOORS

YEAR BUILT

☐ BALCONY   RENOVATIONS NEEDED

☐ GARDEN   ☐

☐ PARKING   ☐

☐ GARAGE   ☐

☐ SWIMMING POOL   ☐

☐ BUILT IN CLOSET ☐

☐ APPLIANCES   ☐

☐ PORCH   ☐

OVERALL CONDITION

WHAT I LIKED   WHAT I DIDN'T LIKE

LOCATION

AGENT   **CONTACT NO.**

DATE FOR VIEWING

PRICE   **SQM**

ROOMS   **FLOORS**

YEAR BUILT

☐ **BALCONY**   **RENOVATIONS NEEDED**

☐ **GARDEN**   ☐

☐ **PARKING**   ☐

☐ **GARAGE**   ☐

☐ **SWIMMING POOL**   ☐

☐ **BUILT IN CLOSET** ☐

☐ **APPLIANCES**   ☐

☐ **PORCH**   ☐

OVERALL CONDITION

WHAT I LIKED   **WHAT I DIDN'T LIKE**

LOCATION

AGENT   CONTACT NO.

DATE FOR VIEWING

PRICE   SQM

ROOMS   FLOORS

YEAR BUILT

- [ ] BALCONY   RENOVATIONS NEEDED
- [ ] GARDEN   [ ]
- [ ] PARKING   [ ]
- [ ] GARAGE   [ ]
- [ ] SWIMMING POOL   [ ]
- [ ] BUILT IN CLOSET   [ ]
- [ ] APPLIANCES   [ ]
- [ ] PORCH   [ ]

OVERALL CONDITION

WHAT I LIKED   WHAT I DIDN'T LIKE

LOCATION

AGENT   **CONTACT NO.**

DATE FOR VIEWING

PRICE   **SQM**

ROOMS   **FLOORS**

YEAR BUILT

- [ ] **BALCONY**   **RENOVATIONS NEEDED**
- [ ] **GARDEN**   [ ]
- [ ] **PARKING**   [ ]
- [ ] **GARAGE**   [ ]
- [ ] **SWIMMING POOL**   [ ]
- [ ] **BUILT IN CLOSET**   [ ]
- [ ] **APPLIANCES**   [ ]
- [ ] **PORCH**   [ ]

OVERALL CONDITION

WHAT I LIKED   **WHAT I DIDN'T LIKE**

LOCATION

AGENT   CONTACT NO.

DATE FOR VIEWING

PRICE   SQM

ROOMS   FLOORS

YEAR BUILT

☐ BALCONY   RENOVATIONS NEEDED
☐ GARDEN   ☐
☐ PARKING   ☐
☐ GARAGE   ☐
☐ SWIMMING POOL   ☐
☐ BUILT IN CLOSET ☐
☐ APPLIANCES   ☐
☐ PORCH   ☐

OVERALL CONDITION

WHAT I LIKED   WHAT I DIDN'T LIKE

LOCATION

AGENT   **CONTACT NO.**

DATE FOR VIEWING

PRICE   **SQM**

ROOMS   **FLOORS**

YEAR BUILT

☐ **BALCONY**   **RENOVATIONS NEEDED**

☐ **GARDEN**   ☐

☐ **PARKING**   ☐

☐ **GARAGE**   ☐

☐ **SWIMMING POOL**   ☐

☐ **BUILT IN CLOSET**   ☐

☐ **APPLIANCES**   ☐

☐ **PORCH**   ☐

OVERALL CONDITION

WHAT I LIKED   **WHAT I DIDN'T LIKE**

LOCATION

AGENT   CONTACT NO.

DATE FOR VIEWING

PRICE   SQM

ROOMS   FLOORS

YEAR BUILT

- [ ] BALCONY   RENOVATIONS NEEDED
- [ ] GARDEN   [ ]
- [ ] PARKING   [ ]
- [ ] GARAGE   [ ]
- [ ] SWIMMING POOL [ ]
- [ ] BUILT IN CLOSET [ ]
- [ ] APPLIANCES   [ ]
- [ ] PORCH   [ ]

OVERALL CONDITION

WHAT I LIKED   WHAT I DIDN'T LIKE

LOCATION

AGENT   **CONTACT NO.**

DATE FOR VIEWING

PRICE   **SQM**

ROOMS   **FLOORS**

YEAR BUILT

- [ ] **BALCONY**   **RENOVATIONS NEEDED**
- [ ] **GARDEN**   [ ]
- [ ] **PARKING**   [ ]
- [ ] **GARAGE**   [ ]
- [ ] **SWIMMING POOL**   [ ]
- [ ] **BUILT IN CLOSET**   [ ]
- [ ] **APPLIANCES**   [ ]
- [ ] **PORCH**   [ ]

OVERALL CONDITION

WHAT I LIKED   **WHAT I DIDN'T LIKE**

LOCATION

AGENT   CONTACT NO.

DATE FOR VIEWING

PRICE   SQM

ROOMS   FLOORS

YEAR BUILT

- ☐ BALCONY
- ☐ GARDEN
- ☐ PARKING
- ☐ GARAGE
- ☐ SWIMMING POOL
- ☐ BUILT IN CLOSET
- ☐ APPLIANCES
- ☐ PORCH

RENOVATIONS NEEDED

☐
☐
☐
☐
☐
☐
☐

OVERALL CONDITION

WHAT I LIKED   WHAT I DIDN'T LIKE

LOCATION

AGENT   **CONTACT NO.**

DATE FOR VIEWING

PRICE   **SQM**

ROOMS   **FLOORS**

YEAR BUILT

- [ ] **BALCONY**   **RENOVATIONS NEEDED**
- [ ] **GARDEN**   [ ]
- [ ] **PARKING**   [ ]
- [ ] **GARAGE**   [ ]
- [ ] **SWIMMING POOL**   [ ]
- [ ] **BUILT IN CLOSET**   [ ]
- [ ] **APPLIANCES**   [ ]
- [ ] **PORCH**   [ ]

OVERALL CONDITION

WHAT I LIKED   **WHAT I DIDN'T LIKE**

LOCATION

AGENT   **CONTACT NO.**

DATE FOR VIEWING

PRICE   **SQM**

ROOMS   **FLOORS**

YEAR BUILT

☐ **BALCONY**   **RENOVATIONS NEEDED**

☐ **GARDEN**   ☐

☐ **PARKING**   ☐

☐ **GARAGE**   ☐

☐ **SWIMMING POOL**   ☐

☐ **BUILT IN CLOSET**   ☐

☐ **APPLIANCES**   ☐

☐ **PORCH**   ☐

OVERALL CONDITION

WHAT I LIKED   **WHAT I DIDN'T LIKE**

LOCATION

AGENT   **CONTACT NO.**

DATE FOR VIEWING

PRICE   **SQM**

ROOMS   **FLOORS**

YEAR BUILT

☐ **BALCONY**   **RENOVATIONS NEEDED**

☐ **GARDEN**   ☐

☐ **PARKING**   ☐

☐ **GARAGE**   ☐

☐ **SWIMMING POOL**   ☐

☐ **BUILT IN CLOSET**   ☐

☐ **APPLIANCES**   ☐

☐ **PORCH**   ☐

OVERALL CONDITION

WHAT I LIKED   **WHAT I DIDN'T LIKE**

LOCATION

AGENT   CONTACT NO.

DATE FOR VIEWING

PRICE   SQM

ROOMS   FLOORS

YEAR BUILT

☐ BALCONY   RENOVATIONS NEEDED
☐ GARDEN   ☐
☐ PARKING   ☐
☐ GARAGE   ☐
☐ SWIMMING POOL   ☐
☐ BUILT IN CLOSET ☐
☐ APPLIANCES   ☐
☐ PORCH   ☐

OVERALL CONDITION

WHAT I LIKED   WHAT I DIDN'T LIKE

LOCATION

AGENT   **CONTACT NO.**

DATE FOR VIEWING

PRICE   **SQM**

ROOMS   **FLOORS**

YEAR BUILT

- [ ] BALCONY   **RENOVATIONS NEEDED**
- [ ] GARDEN   [ ]
- [ ] PARKING   [ ]
- [ ] GARAGE   [ ]
- [ ] SWIMMING POOL   [ ]
- [ ] BUILT IN CLOSET   [ ]
- [ ] APPLIANCES   [ ]
- [ ] PORCH   [ ]

OVERALL CONDITION

WHAT I LIKED   **WHAT I DIDN'T LIKE**

LOCATION

AGENT   CONTACT NO.

DATE FOR VIEWING

PRICE   SQM

ROOMS   FLOORS

YEAR BUILT

- ☐ BALCONY
- ☐ GARDEN
- ☐ PARKING
- ☐ GARAGE
- ☐ SWIMMING POOL
- ☐ BUILT IN CLOSET
- ☐ APPLIANCES
- ☐ PORCH

RENOVATIONS NEEDED

☐
☐
☐
☐
☐
☐

OVERALL CONDITION

WHAT I LIKED   WHAT I DIDN'T LIKE

LOCATION

AGENT   CONTACT NO.

DATE FOR VIEWING

PRICE   SQM

ROOMS   FLOORS

YEAR BUILT

☐ BALCONY   RENOVATIONS NEEDED

☐ GARDEN   ☐

☐ PARKING   ☐

☐ GARAGE   ☐

☐ SWIMMING POOL   ☐

☐ BUILT IN CLOSET   ☐

☐ APPLIANCES   ☐

☐ PORCH   ☐

OVERALL CONDITION

WHAT I LIKED   WHAT I DIDN'T LIKE

LOCATION _____

AGENT _____ CONTACT NO. _____

DATE FOR VIEWING _____

PRICE _____ SQM _____

ROOMS _____ FLOORS _____

YEAR BUILT _____

- ☐ BALCONY
- ☐ GARDEN
- ☐ PARKING
- ☐ GARAGE
- ☐ SWIMMING POOL
- ☐ BUILT IN CLOSET
- ☐ APPLIANCES
- ☐ PORCH

RENOVATIONS NEEDED

☐
☐
☐
☐
☐
☐
☐

OVERALL CONDITION
_____

WHAT I LIKED   WHAT I DIDN'T LIKE
_____
_____
_____
_____
_____
_____

LOCATION

AGENT   CONTACT NO.

DATE FOR VIEWING

PRICE   SQM

ROOMS   FLOORS

YEAR BUILT

☐ BALCONY   RENOVATIONS NEEDED

☐ GARDEN   ☐

☐ PARKING   ☐

☐ GARAGE   ☐

☐ SWIMMING POOL   ☐

☐ BUILT IN CLOSET   ☐

☐ APPLIANCES   ☐

☐ PORCH   ☐

OVERALL CONDITION

WHAT I LIKED   WHAT I DIDN'T LIKE

LOCATION

AGENT   **CONTACT NO.**

DATE FOR VIEWING

PRICE   **SQM**

ROOMS   **FLOORS**

YEAR BUILT

☐ BALCONY   **RENOVATIONS NEEDED**

☐ GARDEN   ☐

☐ PARKING   ☐

☐ GARAGE   ☐

☐ SWIMMING POOL   ☐

☐ BUILT IN CLOSET   ☐

☐ APPLIANCES   ☐

☐ PORCH   ☐

OVERALL CONDITION

WHAT I LIKED   **WHAT I DIDN'T LIKE**

LOCATION

AGENT   **CONTACT NO.**

DATE FOR VIEWING

PRICE   **SQM**

ROOMS   **FLOORS**

YEAR BUILT

- [ ] **BALCONY**   **RENOVATIONS NEEDED**
- [ ] **GARDEN**   [ ]
- [ ] **PARKING**   [ ]
- [ ] **GARAGE**   [ ]
- [ ] **SWIMMING POOL**   [ ]
- [ ] **BUILT IN CLOSET**   [ ]
- [ ] **APPLIANCES**   [ ]
- [ ] **PORCH**   [ ]

OVERALL CONDITION

WHAT I LIKED   **WHAT I DIDN'T LIKE**

LOCATION

AGENT   CONTACT NO.

DATE FOR VIEWING

PRICE   SQM

ROOMS   FLOORS

YEAR BUILT

☐ BALCONY   RENOVATIONS NEEDED
☐ GARDEN   ☐
☐ PARKING   ☐
☐ GARAGE   ☐
☐ SWIMMING POOL   ☐
☐ BUILT IN CLOSET   ☐
☐ APPLIANCES   ☐
☐ PORCH   ☐

OVERALL CONDITION

WHAT I LIKED   WHAT I DIDN'T LIKE

LOCATION

AGENT   **CONTACT NO.**

DATE FOR VIEWING

PRICE   **SQM**

ROOMS   **FLOORS**

YEAR BUILT

- ☐ **BALCONY**   **RENOVATIONS NEEDED**
- ☐ **GARDEN**   ☐
- ☐ **PARKING**   ☐
- ☐ **GARAGE**   ☐
- ☐ **SWIMMING POOL**   ☐
- ☐ **BUILT IN CLOSET**   ☐
- ☐ **APPLIANCES**   ☐
- ☐ **PORCH**   ☐

OVERALL CONDITION

WHAT I LIKED   **WHAT I DIDN'T LIKE**